The FUNNIEST DINOSAUR BOOK EVER!

Joseph Rosenbloom

Illustrated by
Hans Wilhelm

Knock-Knock.
  Who's there?
Dinah.
  Dinah who?

Dinah-saur! Want to hear the funniest
dinosaur jokes ever?

S Sterling Publishing Co., Inc.   New York

NAN: Why are you snapping your fingers?

DAN: To keep the dinosaurs away.

NAN: That's dumb. There are no dinosaurs around here.

DAN: See? It works.

Library of Congress Cataloging-in-Publication Data

Rosenbloom, Joseph.
    The funniest dinosaur book ever!

    Summary: A collection of easy-to-understand jokes and riddles about dinosaurs.
    1. Dinosaurs—Juvenile humor.   2. Wit and humor, Juvenile.   3. Riddles, Juvenile.   [1. Dinosaurs—Wit and humor.   2. Jokes.   3. Riddles]   I. Wilhelm, Hans, 1945–   ill.   II. Title.
PN6231.D65R67   1987   818'.5402   87-7098
ISBN 0-8069-6624-6
ISBN 0-8069-6625-4 (lib. bdg.)

Text copyright © 1987 by Joseph Rosenbloom
Illustrations copyright © 1987 by Hans Wilhelm, Inc.
Published by Sterling Publishing Co., Inc.
Two Park Avenue, New York, N.Y. 10016
Distributed in Canada by Oak Tree Press Ltd.
% Canadian Manda Group, P.O. Box 920, Station U
Toronto, Ontario, Canada M8Z 5P9
Distributed in the United Kingdom by Blandford Press
Link House, West Street, Poole, Dorset BH15 1LL, England
Distributed in Australia by Capricorn Ltd.
P.O. Box 665, Lane Cove, NSW 2066
Manufactured in the United States of America
All rights reserved

What is as big as a dinosaur, but doesn't weigh anything?
The shadow of a dinosaur.

Why did the owl sit on the dinosaur's head?
Because it didn't give a hoot.

Why do you always find dinosaurs on the ground?
Because they won't climb trees.

Why did the dinosaur paint its toenails purple?
So that it could hide in the petunias.

8902387

Where do
dinosaurs go to
swim?
To the dino-shore.

What happens when
a dinosaur dives into
the ocean?
It goes "splash"!

What happens when a green dinosaur goes swimming in the Red Sea?
It gets wet.

How do you keep a dinosaur from smelling?
Put a clothespin on its nose.

What weighs 50 tons, has big teeth and is blue?
A dinosaur holding its breath.

How many dinosaur
skeletons can you put into
an empty museum?
  *One. After that the
  museum isn't empty
  any more.*

Why don't dinosaurs
do well in school?
  *Because their heads
  are so empty.*

Why do little dinosaurs
drink milk?
  *Because milk is good
  for the bones.*

Why is a dinosaur skeleton like a penny?
Because it has a head on one side and a tail on the other.

How do you make a dinosaur skeleton laugh?
Tickle its funny bone.

EXIT

What do you call dinosaur skeletons that sleep all day?
Lazybones.

How do you make a dinosaur stew?

Keep it waiting two hours.

When a dinosaur goes into a restaurant, where does it sit?

Anywhere it wants.

What always follows a dinosaur out of the restaurant?

Its tail.

Why did the dinosaur eat three ducks and a cow?
Because it liked quackers and milk.

How did the dinosaur drink its milkshake?
With a dino-straw.

What does a dinosaur eat with frankfurters and beans?
Dino-slaw.

What two things can't a dinosaur eat for breakfast?
Lunch and dinner.

What would happen if a dinosaur sat in front of you at the movies?
You would miss most of the show.

What dinosaur eats popcorn with its tail?
They all do. No dinosaur takes its tail off to eat popcorn.

What vegetable are you if a dinosaur sits on you?
Squash.

What has a head like a dinosaur, a body like a dinosaur, a tail like a dinosaur—looks just like a dinosaur—but isn't a dinosaur?

A picture of a dinosaur.

How do you get a 100-foot tall dinosaur into a small car?

Open the sun roof.

What is as big as a house, has two legs and twelve wheels?

A dinosaur on roller skates.

How do you get five 100-foot dinosaurs into a small car?

Put two in front, two in back and one in the glove compartment.

How do you run over a
dinosaur?
    *Climb up its neck,
run along its back
and slide down its
tail.*

Why didn't the dinosaur ride a
bicycle?
    *Because it didn't have a
thumb to ring the bell.*

How long should a dinosaur's legs be?
Long enough to reach the ground.

What kind of dinosaur
has red spots?
One with measles.

When does a dinosaur
see as well from either
end?
*When its eyes are
closed.*

What goes, "Thud, thud,
thud—OUCH!"?
A dinosaur with a sore toe.

Which dinosaur wears the biggest cowboy hat?
The one with the biggest head.

What do you call Tyrannosaurus rex when it wears a cowboy hat and boots?
Tyrannosaurus Tex.

What kind of dinosaur can you ride in a rodeo?
A Bronco-saurus (Brontosaurus).

What do you get when
you cross Tyrannosaurus
rex and a chicken?
Tyrannosaurus pecks.

Who is a little
dinosaur's favorite
baby-sitter?
*Ty-granny-
saurus rex.*

What is the hardest thing
about learning to ride a
dinosaur?
The ground.

Why are dinosaurs big,
green and scaly?
*Because if they were
small, white and fuzzy,
they would be tennis balls.*

Why did the dinosaur paint
itself with magic markers?
*So it could hide in the
crayon box.*

Where did the dinosaur buy
its magic markers?
At the dino-store.

What happened when the little dinosaur took the school bus home? *The police made him bring it back.*

$4 + 4 =$

Why shouldn't you add 4 and 4 when you see Tyrannosaurus rex? *Because if you added 4 and 4 you might get 8 (ate).*

How can you tell if a dinosaur is hiding under your bed?
Your nose is close to the ceiling.

What do you call a dinosaur that makes noises when it sleeps?
A dino-snore.

Why did the dinosaur wear purple pajamas?
His pink ones were in the wash.

MOTHER: Junior, what do you mean by bringing that 100-foot-long dinosaur into your room?

JUNIOR: It's all right, mom. I'm only going to keep him overnight.

How can you tell if a dinosaur is in your bed?
By the big D on its pajamas.

Why do dinosaurs lie down?
Because they can't lie up.

Why are dinosaurs invited to parties?
Because they are tons of fun.

How does a magician
cut a dinosaur in two?
With a dino-saw.

When does a
dinosaur look like a
cute little clown?
*When it wears its
cute little clown
suit.*

MAGIC

What time is it when you meet Tyrannosaurus rex at a party?
Time to run.

What goes "Ho, ho, ho, ho— PLOP!"?
A dinosaur laughing its head off.

Who won the dinosaur beauty contest?
No one.

What do you sing to a dinosaur when it's 70 million years old?
"Happy birthday to you. . . ."

Why did the dinosaur
wear dark glasses?
  *With all these
  dinosaur jokes, it
  didn't want to be
  recognized.*

Why did the dinosaur
become extinct?
  *It didn't want to hear
  any more dinosaur
  jokes.*